STOP: Get Ready To Re-Invent Yourself

How To Prepare Yourself For Lasting Life Change

By John-Paul Byrne

Copyright © 2020. All Rights Reserved.

Book #1 in the *STOP. START. RE-INVENT: How To Re-Invent Yourself & Create Lasting Change In Your Life* series.

Copyright Notice

STOP: Get Ready To Re-Invent Yourself
How To Prepare Yourself For Lasting Life Change

© 2020 John-Paul Byrne All rights reserved.

No part of this publication may be reproduced, stored in a retrieval system or transmitted by any means - electronic, mechanical, photographic (photocopying). recording, or otherwise without the prior permission in writing from the author, except as permitted by U.K copyright law.

For permissions contact: info@StopStartReInvent.com

Disclaimer: The information provided in this book is designed to provide helpful information on the subjects discussed from the author's own experience and knowledge. This book is not meant to be used, nor should it be used, to diagnose or treat any medical or mental health condition. For diagnosis or treatment of any medical problem or mental health issue, consult your own physician. The publisher and author are not responsible for any aspect of your physical or mental health and are not liable for any damages or negative consequences from any treatment, action, application or preparation, to any person reading or following the information in this book. References are provided for informational purposes only and do not constitute endorsement of any websites or other sources.

Published by John-Paul International Ltd International House, 12 Constance Street, London, United Kingdom, E16 2DQ

ISBN: 9798639705090 (Paperback Format)
www.StopStartReInvent.com

Image Cover/Credits: Images courtesy of canva.com.
Cover design by John-Paul Byrne.
Last Updated 26th May 2020

This book is dedicated to Chris & Mel. You have always reminded me of who I am when I got lost and helped me get back up again.

Thank you for your kindness and friendship.

Get Book #2

in the
STOP. START. RE-INVENT series

Thank you for putting your faith in me and purchasing this book.

STOP: Get Ready To Re-Invent Yourself is the first book in the series ***STOP. START. RE-INVENT: How To Re-Invent Yourself & Create Lasting Change In Your Life***

The next book in this series is called:

START: Begin Your Personal Re-Invention Today

Please visit the link below to get your copy of the second book in this series in either paperback, kindle or audible formats

https://go.stopstartreinvent.com/SSR01B2/buy

I would be most grateful if you could leave a review on Amazon so that others looking to make lasting change in their life can benefit from this series.

I wish you inner peace, joy and enthusiasm
as you embark on your personal re-invention

- John-Paul Byrne, Peterborough, UK

Contents

Get Book #2 7
Preface 13
Introduction 21
What is Personal Re-Invention? 27
    Is this book for Me? 27
    How much pain is too much pain? 28
    Change: Reactive or Pro-active? 30
    Should I abandon my life tomorrow? 32
    What can You expect from this book? 33
STOP 35
    Story: The One Pound Coin 35
    Are you ploughing on without looking up? 38
    Visualisation Technique for Stopping: Train on Track 39
    Making a different choice 41
    My STOP state 42
    Summary 44
    Techniques 44
    Useful Resources 44
Observe 45
    Ego and self-awareness 45
    Awkward Conversations 47
    Story: Table Twenty-Nine 48
    Technique for observing yourself: Ego Neutralizer 49

Visualisation Technique for removing negative emotions: The Window and Me 51
    Summary 52
    Techniques 52
    Useful Resources 53

Patience 55
    The Weighing Station 55
    Why do we quit on ourselves? 56
    Generation: Instant 57
    The Bus and You 59
    Too impatient for success 60
    Driving at night 61
    Patience and Motivation 62
    Summary 62
    Useful Resources 63

Certainty 65
    Self-belief is abstract 65
    Technique for certainty: A Certain Outcome 68
    Certainty got me results 69
    Story: The Red Hammer 70
    A compelling reason 71
    A reason why 71
    Summary 72
    Techniques 73
    Useful Resources 73

Fear 75

- The fears we have 75
- Unlimited Possibility 77
- Technique for creating "musts": Walk Past Your Fears .. 77
- Story: A Song in My Head 79
- The Universal Fear 81
- Keep moving forward 81
- Summary 82
- Techniques 82
- Useful Resources 83

Love 85
- What is love? Baby don't hurt me. 85
- The pursuit of happiness 86
- Defining relationships 88
- Story: Poor Me! 88
- Technique for two: Relationship evaluation 89
- A shared vision 90
- Summary 91
- Techniques 91
- Useful Resources 91

Lows 93
- What's the point? 94
- Low Labels 95
- Fighting Depression? 96
- The Depressed Mind 98
- Roses and Lollipops 98

Technique for dealing with depression or sadness: Send Yourself a Message 99
    Looking Low 100
    Moving forward, looking back 101
    Summary 102
    Techniques 102
    Useful Resources 103
Get Ready To START 105
Author Summary 107
Acknowledgements 109
About the Author 113
Get Book #2 115
Leave a Review 117
Other Books In This Series 119
    Book #2 119
    Book #3 120
Appendix 121

Preface

There is nothing to stop you from achieving anything
- John-Paul Byrne, 2014

Hello. My name is John-Paul Byrne. I am thirty-six years old as I write this and I live in Peterborough, England. I have two young children, a boy and a girl.

I started writing this book for a reason and that reason is to help myself as much as it is to help you. I spent the past few months wondering why I am lonely, depressed and broke at the age of thirty-six.

Have you have had those days when you feel like you're a total disaster? The days when you feel like you are just not where you thought you would be?

Well that's where you find me now.

I work a full-time job contracting myself out to companies, developing software. It pays well but for the life of me, I'm not sure why I'm still broke. I've been living in this house a few months now and to be honest, I am struggling a bit. I've recently come out of a three-year relationship and find myself living on my own.

I see my two children regularly. In between work and the children, I often find myself here at the dining room table trying to figure out where it all went wrong.

This is not the life I had planned in my twenties or rather, if I had planned my life in my twenties, then it certainly would not have looked like this!

I love my kids but there is something missing. I find myself trying to figure out why my relationships never seem to work among a myriad of other things:

Why do I always feel down and lost?
Why am I broke?
Why do I feel not good enough?
What is this emptiness inside me?
Why am I just not where I want to be in life?
Why don't I like the way I look?
When am I going to do something good?
Why am I living just to work and make money?

Maybe you've felt like this at one time or another? Today however, I decided to ask myself a better question:

What did I do in the past to change my life?

I had survived sleeping rough on intermittent occasions in England, abandoned by my mother. I survived that.

I managed to re-invent myself and achieve six A-levels after those experiences, in the same time people did three. I had beaten all the odds and achieved something far beyond even my own expectations.

I applied to Cambridge to study Law at the age of eighteen and they said, *"Come back when you have twenty-eight points Mr Byrne"*. So just to be awkward, I came back with forty-fix, pretty much top marks in the country for that year.

I hate to disappoint though: they still wouldn't have me. Maybe it was my haircut? Who knows?

I survived losing my business a year after getting married and starting again. I had survived divorce (yep my fault!) and turned it into friendship.

I had learned how to survive depression, mania and the diagnosis of Bipolar Disorder so I could still be a decent Dad and hold down a job.

I had survived an emotionally and physically abusive mother yet never held any anger towards her (or so I thought).

I sat and wondered:

What were the techniques that I had used to come through these experiences? How could I use these very same techniques again to even greater effect to create a better life, one that I really wanted?

That's what this book is about.

Here is my logic: If I can remember what I've done in the past to change my situation then I can apply the same strategy to my current reality and move forward. Better still, I could write it down, maybe systemise it, put it all in this book and help you create lasting change in *your* life.

Let's be honest, my life is not at all bad at present, but everything is relative. You don't have to destitute or live in a third world country to be unhappy. You might just be unhappy and that's enough of a reason to want to change your life.

So, what is my strategy for changing your life when you are not happy with your current circumstances?

It's called "**STOP. START. RE-INVENT.**"

It's the simplest way I could describe how I had changed my life in the past, despite it feeling completely impossible at the time.

Most of us cannot conceive a reality that we have not yet experienced. That's about to change for us both.

My motivation comes primarily from a background of emotional and physical abuse, manic-depression, homelessness, divorce, self-destruction, love, fatherhood, entrepreneurship, learning and mistakes.

However, I always thought there was a lot more to me than that. You probably feel the same about yourself.

You could do more, be more, achieve more.

In twenty-twelve I became a Certified Practitioner in Life Coaching, NLP, Hypnosis and I completed Time Line Therapy training.

I wanted to do something that felt like it was going to have a positive impact on others. Sadly, I never managed to turn it into a career and still found myself writing code for a living.

That is where this story and the "**STOP. START. RE-INVENT.**" strategy begins.

I also have a degree in Computer Science from Southampton University. I have run companies from the age of twenty, not necessarily successfully, but it's still worth me noting it down as a personal achievement.

I stayed in Malibu on a working holiday at the age of twenty as Chief Technology Officer for a health firm - just two years after having nowhere to live whilst completing my high school.

Since then, I have worked for some of the world's biggest companies.

I think I have been kind to people over the years. I am pretty sure I have been caring. I have made lots of money and I have lost plenty of it through reckless management, impatience and immaturity.

I have loved and I have lost. I have made mistakes and I have plenty of past trauma that is probably about to bite me in the ass!

However, what I am good at is system design. I'm very good at figuring out how to give people simple step-by-step strategies to solve problems. I built my career on translating people's needs into software. I am both overly emotional and insanely logical. I am a master at creating models in my head for pretty much everything. This has its pros and cons as you shall discover.

Can models and strategies be applied to the complexity of changing one's life though?

Yes, it can.

That's why I am excited about this book. I know it's possible to re-invent yourself and it doesn't have to take forever.

When I sat down and really considered what I wanted to give you through this book, I realised it was inspiration.

I want to inspire *You* to re-invent yourself using the strategies and mindset that I used to create change for myself. If this book empowers and teaches only one single person to re-invent themselves then it will have been worth it.

I find that most days are a war between the John-Paul who is a lazy thinker and would prefer to give up and the other John-Paul who is the one writing this book. The latter JP is the one pulling me up, never letting me fall too far. He's coaching me, inspiring me to use what I know and what I have experienced to re-invent myself and share that journey with others.

He's the guy that says:

Accept the now, pick yourself up and start again!

This is an honest book. It's not pretend ideal world bullshit. It's also not another run-of-the-mill self-development book because it's going to include my progress as I am re-inventing my life. You will get to see first-hand, **STOP. START. RE-INVENT** in action.

This should not be a book that *You* buy, read, yet put down and lead the same old life you did before. This is your call to action book. If you are reading this book, then I know that you want to change or improve your current situation.

You do, right?

So, let's just set the background scene together. As I write, I still work a normal job. I love my job, but I've always had this gut feeling that I should lead or inspire people to do good stuff with their life. However, when your own life looks a mess, it's time to work on yourself first. That's where I am starting from.

I am a software engineer. I think I am very good at it otherwise I suspect I would have been fired at least once! It pays well and it's stable but being a software engineer is not what I really want to do in my life.

By the time you finish reading this book I may not have "made it". I might still be coding software or better still I might have a completely new life.

Here is an exciting thought:

What will be the next twist or turn ahead and better still, how can I create the change in my life that I really want?

Stability doesn't always yield the expectations we had for ourselves. We need it but we can learn to work with it. That's the theme of this book.

There is no bungy jumping off Big Ben or believing you can win the lottery by Saturday. There will be no driving down the motorway into the sunset without enough petrol or your wallet.

Despite being impulsive, a risk taker and often having a "fuck it" attitude, I owe it to you to write sensible, implementable, real world guidance for creating the re-invented *You*.

For me, it's got to be realistic, especially if I am going to ask *You* to apply it to your life. What's in this book is honest, probably rough around the edges and it's from my heart.

Join me on our journey and allow yourself to be surprised by *You* and what you can achieve by implementing the guidance in this book.

I think I made this quote up but either way, it's just popped into my head, so here it is:

You are not where you are today. You are where you decided to be yesterday.

Introduction

Are you unhappy with your life? Do you find yourself stuck in a rut? Maybe you find yourself wishing for something more? Do you feel that life has dealt you an unlucky hand or that your current reality is simply not your fault?

It's OK, you are not alone. Millions of people feel trapped in their current situation, unable to create lasting change in their life or have the success they say they want.

Maybe you have attempted to move forward with best laid plans and yet fall right back into your old life all too quickly?

STOP: Get Ready To Re-Invent Yourself, How To Prepare Yourself For Lasting Life Change, is written exactly for You.

What most people do not realise is that the change they think they want is not going to magically happen.

It will not come from winning the lottery, meeting that beautiful woman, having that big house, getting that pay rise or any other external act from the universe, which many wait for helplessly.

What's sad is that most people never truly find the courage to change their situation. They are not exposed to self-development and they probably have no idea of the benefits of a coach or mentor.

Worse still, they are surrounded by people who are experiencing the same reality. They are trapped in unhealthy environments, often addicted to the same vices of bad diet, TV, porn, grumbling and poisonous negative emotions whilst destroying their health.

Many beautiful souls have lost their spark, submitting to a sense of drudgery and victimhood that secures them with a lifetime of discontent.

Bronnie Ware, a nurse who cared for terminally ill patients, wrote about the #1 thing people say when they are dying. She revealed they said:

> *"I wish I'd had the courage to live a life true to myself, not the life others expected of me".*

So, will you be another statistic of the graveyard of "could haves", "should haves" and "why did I nots"?

Before you run out the front door, quit your job, leave your unhappy relationship or sail off into the sunset, there is a kicker: You must prepare yourself for lasting change, otherwise you will keep falling back to where you find yourself right now.

This book is the first book in the three-part series:

STOP. START. RE-INVENT: How To Re-Invent Yourself & Create Lasting Change In Your Life

I have had plenty of problems and past trauma, much like most. I also have great things in my life, much like most. However, I was unhappy and frustrated that my thoughts never really changed. I found myself trapped in bad habits, a shitty mindset, repeating the same patterns of behaviour and all the while getting tired and older.

I wasn't where I thought I should be in life.

Have you ever felt like this?

I was certainly not being the best version of myself or in alignment with my soul purpose.

From a place of depression, I decided to look back at the events in my life where I had unknowingly created lasting change. Through my writings on personal re-invention in this three-part series, I reveal how I re-invented my life, changed my environment, my mindset, my wealth and the value I bring to the world and how you can too.

I became an international speaker, won awards for my ideas and began to help others.

Across the three books in this series, I share my strategies, techniques and the self-talk which enabled me to create lasting change, discover myself, my true calling and a love for writing.

By re-inventing myself from the inside out, I found myself working with global thought leaders, making a positive impact in the world. I found that by changing my environment and the energy that comes into my life, I could create lasting change.

This is not a book about starting a business or how to achieve wealth and recognition, although these things could be a natural side effect of reading it and other books in the series.

Neither is this book a pre-cursor to a journey of success that will be complete for either You or I, because our growth never stops.

STOP: Get Ready To Re-Invent Yourself is a very different book. It's not a self-development book that preaches advice that I have no experience or evidence of implementing. Instead, this book is a step-by-step, easy-to-follow guide to prepare you for lasting life change.

You are going to learn how to STOP, reflect and re-think about who You are and where You are presently at. This book is going to teach you how to prepare your mind for the success you desire and the exciting journey ahead.

By reading it, you will discover, sharpen and perhaps totally re-write what you really want and how you show up in the world. This preparation is essential before you get started on your personal re-invention.

The second book in this series, *START: Begin Your Personal Re-Invention Today* will take you on the next stage of your journey AFTER you have done the necessary groundwork revealed in this first book.

Within all books in this series, I write with vulnerability and openness as I reveal parts of my own journey, mistakes, struggles and realisations.

Follow me on this journey and witness how the decisions and tiny changes I made, created dramatic positive changes in my life.

Don't be fooled. This series does not end with a story of a big bank balance and a huge success that is a million miles from most people's life.

Instead, You, the reader, will be taken on a journey towards a beautiful lesson which I endured as I wrote and systemised the path to lasting life change.

Your personal re-invention awaits You.

What is Personal Re-Invention?

I think it's this:

> *Personal Re-Invention is turning yourself, your life and your mind into the You that you've always wanted. It's having the guts to be relentless, to take charge of your life, define and fulfil your mission. It's about becoming who you truly are. It's having the balls to stand up and say: "No more will I be less than I am capable of. No more will I accept a living that is less than my vision."*
>
> *- John-Paul Byrne, 2014*

Is this book for Me?

Let's set the context. Who is this book for? It is for *You*. Are you living the life you wanted? Are you unable to achieve lasting change in your life? Are you constantly failing to start what you know you should be doing?

Are you constantly giving up on yourself in the first yard? Have you lost hope in yourself because every time you try, it seems to end in failure?

Have you given up on your vision or your dreams? Do you wish there was something that could enable you to achieve more happiness and results in your life with less pain?

I do.

This book is for anyone whose life does not match the blueprint they have in their head. My life does not match the blueprint in my head which is exactly why I am writing this book.

We all have aspects of our life which have not turned out the way we expected. We all have areas of our life we want to work on, yet another year goes by and we are still in the same situation.

Therefore, this book is written for *You*.

There are ideas in this book that will enable you to *re-invent* yourself. There are techniques and insights that will enable you to create the best possible blueprint to improve your life.

> *Stop. Start. Re-Invent is a wake-up call for "Personal Re-Invention". You are as you are right now, but you can be all the things you want to be.*

How much pain is too much pain?

What is it going to take for you to stand up and say:

> "No more will I settle for less. No more will I settle for the way I am. No more will I accept this way of living when it's not the living I had dreamed of"?

What level of pain will you have to experience to stand up and take charge of your life?

What will you have to do to become the best version of *You* that you know you can be?

What are the words you will have to hear to change your thinking and stop quitting on yourself?

What is it that has to happen for you to define your *life* and live it?

It's true: time is running out to do the things you said you would and time is running out for you to be the person you know you can be.

Although I feel twenty-eight years old in my head, I feel like I'm running out of time, wrapped up in the problems and aspects of my life that just don't work for me.

How do you feel?

Maybe you are in an unhappy relationship or have poor health, living hand to mouth or suffering from addiction, depression, low self-esteem and fear?

Maybe you are unhappy with your career or your finances?

We all have something that is just not working for us and we all have a story that we tell ourselves; the story that explains all these things. I learned that my current story will not build me a new future unless I change my story and match that with different actions.

There was no promise at the beginning of our life that it would be a walk in the park. Everyone has problems and it's said that problems are life. Seems a bit bleak to me because I think there is more to life than just *problems*.

I think that once we accept that life can be so much more than problem after problem, it enables us to start looking forward. It's the constant pushing against the resistance that turns us into new people with new insights and new abilities

It's this same pushing which gives us life and in the gaps, we find happiness, peace, love, appreciation and all those things that we expected to land in our laps without any effort.

Change: Reactive or Pro-active?

Whether we like it or not, the changes that we experience are often unconscious, relentless and delivered every second. What if together, we could start ordering the exact changes we want?

This book is written for *You* as a tool to create the change that you want in your life. Change is inevitable for everyone so why do we let it happen to us instead of creating the change we want? By making a conscious decision to invest in yourself you can get the outcomes, the circumstances and the results that you want.

How many times has your inner voice said "I am going to...., I will start to ..., I want to be ..." but you and your life just get in the way and you go bouncing from side to side?

We tell ourselves "I could never..." or "I would but...". It's time to change that inner dialogue.

I want you to use what's in this book and apply it to your life. Unlock your inner child's passion to be alive and move yourself forward in the direction that you want. I always remember the line "Life is not a rehearsal" so just do it anyway.

If we want a different reality, then we must stop bouncing around. There is only one chance. That chance is *Your Life*. Don't do what so many have done before you - find yourself in your last hours saying, "I could have done so much more, what was I scared of?" You are the only person in the entire universe that was given your dream; your vision of *You*.

No matter who you are or what your situation, you can re-invent yourself. Personal re-invention is just that - it is personal to you.

People can turn their lives around, their careers, beat depression, illness, overcome dire personal circumstances and abuse, educate themselves, become wealthy, successful or simply commit every day to walking to work.

It's not the size of the change that counts, it's the fact that you made it possible.

The race is only with yourself. Your challenges and desires are personal to you. What is a huge re-invention to one person may be a simple task for another, so resist the temptation to compare *You* to anyone else whose thoughts you can't read.

I used to be a mind-reader but I got fired due to translation issues.

The commonality in all personal reinvention is the achievement of the outcomes that we want. It's the achievement and knowing that says:

I am the me I planned for, I am no longer the me that got here as result of random acts of universal change.

So, stop watching mindless TV, drinking endless amounts of coffee, telling yourself *"I am too tired"*.

If you are tired now how much more tired will you be a year from now or in ten years' time?

Ask yourself:

This time last year, or even four years ago, was your life mostly the same? Did you have the same vision during those years and yet still find you have not achieved any or all of it?

Should I abandon my life tomorrow?

Let's be clear on one thing. Re-inventing yourself is not about pursuing a new life at the expense of the things in your life that are good, that are right, that are precious. You cannot re-invent yourself by discarding the critical assets you already have.

You cannot discard important aspects such as your family, love, kindness, giving time to your children or your partner. Those assets that *do* match perfectly with your blueprint should be held onto and remain integral to who you are.

We won't be turning at a right angle away from all the things that you have built in your life, which are in alignment with what you want. We will be learning to work with them, to knit them into your new reality.

Remember that you are not alone in your personal re-invention. This book documents my own personal re-invention.

This is a journey. It is simple but it won't be easy and that's exactly why you haven't re-invented yourself yet. It's tough, it requires resilience, determination, passion and fun in the process.

This is my blueprint, this is how I am re-inventing myself, this is how I have done it in the past.

What can You expect from this book?

One of the gifts this book will give you is a wider mindset.

Experts are only experts in what they know and that concludes they do not know everything. This statement certainly includes me.

I am going to expose you to other people who have inspired me, other people I have learned from. There will be parts of this book where the message is not original. There will be plenty of references to the people who inspire me. I will share with you who they are and where to find their best material.

Are you ready? We will do this together. We are on board. You are already amazing. Now let's smash it.

Remember that this is the first book in the **STOP. START. RE-INVENT** series. The other two books cover the **START** and the **RE-INVENT** aspects of personal re-invention.

You can download resources for this book at:

https://go.stopstartreinvent.com/resources/SSR01B1

STOP
Chapter One

The definition of insanity is doing the same thing over and over again and expecting a different result
- Albert Einstein

Stop thinking. Impossible, right? So, what is this first step of personal re-invention? It seems counter-intuitive to need to stop what you are doing and what you are thinking.

The need to *do* and *progress* seems more important now that we have decided to re-invent ourselves. The need to do more and to work even harder, investing more time and more effort, might seem like the best solution to our problems.

I want to tell you a story.

Story: The One Pound Coin

When I was in my early twenties, I had my own software company. It was small, but the products were good. I spent a long time building the software. I had a vision that I wanted to provide real solutions to businesses. I wanted my customers to be happy. I was brilliant at selling the software. I was brilliant at writing it. Everything about it seemed perfect and made complete sense to me.

I had committed everything I had to my company which included all my money. I had risked my inheritance, taken loans against my house, credit cards, overdrafts, the lot. I was certain it would all work out successfully. I worked ridiculous hours; coding through the night; driving hundreds of miles to train people without sleep and pushing blindly forward every day. I never looked up. I was silently killing myself.

There was literally nothing else in my life that I was paying attention to. The initial ideas of "great at selling", "great at producing software" had blinded me completely.

It was a Friday evening and I was sat in my office alone. It was dark outside. The numbers were up. It was over. A knock came at my office door. It was the director of a company whom I had pitched to a week or so earlier. He came in, sat opposite to me and asked me how I was. He knew the director of my biggest client. He knew that my company was going under.

Taking out his wallet, he put five twenties on the table and a one-pound coin.

"The one pound is from James (my biggest client) for the rights to all your software, your intellectual property and a job working for him with relocation on thirty-five thousand per year. The five twenties are for you as a gift from me. If you take my money, I want you to go home, get some rest and take your wife out for dinner.

A few years ago, I was in the same situation as you. I had nothing left and somebody did the same for me. You have worked incredibly hard and your company has failed. You need to consider why from being successful at what you do, you have arrived at this. This experience will be essential for the rest of your life. What will you choose?"

I sat back in my chair in utter astonishment. I had not been expecting this. James owed me thousands and had the audacity to send a message like this. I stared at the one-pound coin. It presented a financial solution when my back was against the wall. I looked at the five twenties that represented a chance to get up and walk away and start again.

I reached slowly over the table eyeing the one-pound coin, scooped up the twenties and put them in my pocket. He smiled at me, tossing the one pound in the air before placing it in his inside jacket pocket. "Take care John-Paul" he said as he got up and left.

I never saw him again. This kindness genuinely touched me.

I was immensely grateful for what he had done. I did not have one pound to my name. It was ghastly. But this man had given me far more than one hundred pounds. It was not until that moment, that evening, I realized I had not stopped over the last few years.

I had not stopped to cross check the narrative I was telling myself. I had not stopped in my business to look up and deal with the real facts about price, investment, partnering. I had not stopped to assess the destruction of myself in the pursuit of my vision. It had cost me everything.

There is much I have learned from my first business failure but stopping has been the most empowering lesson.
Whatever it is you are going through right now it's probably painful. I don't know where that pain is in your life. You do.

Stop.

It is essential to gain objectivity; an external view of your current situation.

Are you ploughing on without looking up?

You might be ploughing on forward trying to lose weight and failing. You might be ploughing on forward expecting your partner to change, your relationship to improve.

You might be ploughing on forward shouting, screaming at your kids, wondering why it has no effect.

You might be ploughing on forward in a job you hate with knowledge you could apply to your own business or a more fulfilling career.

You might be ploughing on forward expecting success and fulfilment to just land in your lap.

So, what techniques can we use to get to the "Stop" state so that we can begin again and start a journey of personal re-invention?

The technique below is powerful. You should read and re-read it. Know it intensely. Commit to this. You will use it at any time in your life to stop on your current track. It has worked for me. It will work for you. Accept this. Benefit from it. It is the beginning of the path that will produce the results you want in your life.

Visualisation Technique for Stopping: Train on Track

Find somewhere quiet to sit or lie down. Make sure it is comfortable. If you have a noisy house and kids running around, then do this when they are asleep. If you have a particularly demanding partner who doesn't understand that you need to take this time for yourself, then explain to them that you need half an hour of quiet relaxation.

They may surprise you and understand. Essentially make sure you will not be disturbed and that you are in a quiet room. This is time for you, and you need it.

Love yourself enough to take this time. Enjoy.

```
Imagine you are on a train. You are sitting
in a warm and comfortable seat next to the
window. You look out of the window and see
the hedges, trees and fields whizzing past;
faster than you have time to determine their
full detail. The sun is shining and you feel
content. The speed and swiftness of the
train is empowering. You do not remember at
which station you joined the train and you
do not wish to leave the train. It is safe
and warm in your carriage and you are
familiar with your window seat. Close your
eyes and feel this for a moment.
```

Now, you are ready to see *You* on the train from a different perspective.

I want you to imagine that you can float high up into the sky or sideways or forwards or backwards. You are free to float where you want. I want you to see yourself sitting in the window seat. Float upwards from your body, above the train carriage. You can now see the roof of the train carriage at your feet. You are perfectly safe. You are still sitting by the window, but your imagination is following my instructions.

Float higher now until the carriage and the train start to become smaller beneath you and then float higher again. It is peaceful and free where you are. You can see the train below you zooming along it's track. As you look up the track you notice it forks.

One of the rails leads far into the distance with no stations visible. The train will not come to a stop on that route.

You notice the other rail has a station stop. There will be the option to change trains at this station or simply to get off the train and take a break. You are powerful and have the choice which rail the train will go down. Use your mind to tell the train driver the track to choose.

Keep your eyes closed and think of this now and be silent. I will see you back here in a moment.

Making a different choice

If you choose the rail with the unknown station you are ready to take complete charge of your life. You just took control. You did this by yourself.

If you have chosen the rail route with no station then this is ok too. You are content on your journey and like having stability and continuity. You are subconsciously being controlled by your fear of change however. So, revisit the technique again many times over the next few days and allow yourself to be open to the idea of stopping at the other station.

Imagine your life is this train. Nobody else should be concerned with where your train is headed. It is speeding along the track, your life, with the same regular, predictable direction. The rail that stretched out into the distance with no stations will not produce a different result in your life.

A conscious decision to choose the rail that stops at the station will lead to a very different outcome. This an undeniable truth you know.

You have no idea what the station is called or which other trains you can choose at that station, but this is ok. Choose to let go of the predictable route and be certain that getting the outcomes you want will start at the unknown station. You can explore this station and make decisions about where you want to go even if it means you choose to go back onto the old rail route.

Imagine the train stopping at this unknown station. Use your imagination to see how nice it is and all the happy smiling faces on the platform. You don't recognize them, but they seem connected to you. They are just like you. They have taken charge by stopping at this station too.

The visualization of the train speeding along below you is a technique you can use any time to look at your life from the outside in an objective, unemotional way. This technique allows you to take control and make the choice to mentally *stop*. Leave all feelings on the train and just look at the facts.

Train on Track is the technique I want you to do today. The unknown station is exactly where you are in your life right now. The unknown station is this book. You can reinforce your commitment to a different version of *You* by doing this technique. Now this is not hard is it?

I promised you simplicity. You can of course trust in simplicity.

I want to share with you my unknown station, remembering of course that we are both embarking on our own personal re-inventions. I promised you this book was not ideal-world bullshit.

It is a living journey for me and for you.

My STOP state

Ever since I was young, I wanted to help others and speak to groups of people. I saw myself doing this from a young age, but I was not sure why. This desire was strong inside me. Most of my actions were motivated by this desire. Few of those actions were successful.

Many of my actions often resulted in unplanned personal self-sabotage. So far, as I write this chapter, I haven't realised my dream of inspiring other people to live the life they want, or have I?

I am now thirty-six and I have had two long term relationships that have not worked out and I continue to work in software development. This was not what I had planned because, in fact, I hadn't really planned anything.

Despite how grateful I am for the job I do and the people I work with, I don't want to develop software for the rest of my life. I don't want to repeat the same mistakes in my future relationships. I want to take better care of my health and fitness.

I want to take control of my finances with sustainable business. I want to help people from a position of personal strength. I want to inspire people to make choices that get the results they want. I want to embark on a journey that matches the passion inside.

How am I going to do that?

I have my **Stop** state. What is yours? You now know me a little better.

Let's move forward together.

Summary

- You cannot gain objectivity about your life whilst continuing to do what you have always done
- Sometimes the easiest choice is not the right one because it can unwittingly leave you on the same path.
- Taking time out for yourself to do a simple visualisation technique shows that you can love yourself
- Stopping means making a different choice than the one you continue to make every day

Techniques

- The *Train on Track* is a dissociative visualisation technique to gain a different perspective on your life and open your mind to other possibilities

Useful Resources

- You can also download the *Train on Track* audio from

    https://go.stopstartreinvent.com/SSR01B1/resources/stop

Observe
Chapter Two

If you stood at the edge of a cliff, would you see the waves crashing below or would you see yourself at the beginning of a large slab of rock that stretches endlessly behind you?

- *John-Paul Byrne - 2015*

If we saw ourselves as other people see us, how long would it take us to recognize all the greatness in ourselves? How long would it take us to recognize the parts of our life we could change which are in conflict with who we really are? How soon would we recognize the opportunities that lie all around us, just like that slab of rock by the cliff?

Why do we need to be able to observe ourselves to start our personal re-invention?

For me, its purpose has been to gain acceptance of who I am. Acceptance of the good and the bad and of all actions I have taken. It is essential to assess who I have been and be at peace with the here and the now. It is essential to let go of what has gone before and what has been done before. It is gaining the acceptance that things are just as they are right now.

Ego and self-awareness

This next phase in your personal re-invention is to understand the value of self-observation. Maybe you are *chomping at the bit* and want to get to the stuff you think will be in the next chapters. You need to trust in the importance of this process and commit to mastering what is in this chapter first. We are in the "Stop" state now. It is for you.

I was inspired by Eckart Tolle's book, "A New Earth". His message in a very short summary is:

Our ego runs our life and our mind. Our ego's sole purpose is to survive. Observing our ego leads us to realize that it is the outward driving force of all that we do. This is the same ego that constantly narrates your reality. It's the ego that relies on outward confirmation of success to bolster itself. It's the ego that thrives on being better than others. It's the ego that wants to be loved. It's the ego that gets jealous or angry when it's not in control.

Silencing our mind with absolutely no thought allows us to observe who we are. It allows us to be present in every situation. It allows us to observe ourselves without judgement.

This presence in self, diminishes the ego and allows us to discover that we are a conscious being of limitless potential.

In Eckhart's words:

Stop searching for happiness and you'll realize where it is - in those moments and feelings that you can't put into words.

I was always so consumed with "*doing*". I was unaware that I could learn how to step back from my own ego and observe myself. The self-awareness to step back from the internal chatter took some time to root itself in me. But then one day it dawned on me. Just like the visualization of myself on the train, I was able to step back from myself and feel an enormous sense of peace and space inside the chaos of my own life.

The true journey of discovery does not consist of searching for new landscapes, but in having new eyes. – Marcel Proust

If we are going to judge the possibilities for our future based on our current circumstances, the game is up and we will continue to get the results we have always got.

Awkward Conversations

How often have you met someone you know, perhaps while you are shopping or walking the dog and left the conversation feeling conflicted? The conversation that falls out of our mouth with no planning is often spoken with little self-awareness.

These conversations often leave you saying to yourself "Oh, why did I say that? That's not what I meant. Oh, I feel really silly now."

How many times have you reacted hastily to the response you have interpreted from someone because you felt bad, awkward or embarrassed?

Your ego is the voice inside your head to be observed and controlled. Controlling it empowers you to manage your emotions and take a step back before you jump into situations. Managing the voice inside your head enables you to be present in any situation so that you can communicate clearly.

Observe your thoughts when you talk to others who doubt your ability to achieve the results that you want. The people who have told you that you could never do *this* or *that*. Those people who look at you and you think they don't believe a word of your vision. What you think they think of you is only your thinking.

The response you perceive from others may not be the only truth. The response is a reflection of your feelings which you are projecting. Feelings of self-doubt and fear radiate from us all the time.

Emotional awareness and emotional control are a by-product of observing yourself. So how can we learn to observe our chattering thoughts and get control of our ego?

I want to tell you a story.

Story: Table Twenty-Nine

I went to a restaurant with my two children. Sunday dinner plus children's activity play area all under one roof. Every parents dream!

The entrance to the seating area was quiet. I stood there by the "wait here to be seated" sign for a long fifteen seconds before I ushered the kids down among the tables. We happily decided on the best table based on proximity to play area. We choose table twenty-nine.

Just as I was about to take off my coat the waiter came and asked me if I was ok. "Yes, I'm fine thanks".

He then said "Many of these tables are reserved and therefore we have a hosted seating service. I will need to check if this table is free for you".

I quickly replied, "I didn't see anyone about, so we are taking this table." Despite knowing I was probably in the wrong, I sat down. During my usual game of i-spy with the children, I started to feel rather guilty. I stood outside myself and thought about the earlier conversation and asked myself the following questions.

1. What is the first feeling that came into my head about the event? Embarrassed.
2. Why specifically did I feel embarrassed? I knew there was a seating service, but I had been too impatient to wait.
3. What did I look like with this feeling? Probably rude and uncaring.
4. What did I say to myself when I felt this feeling? I've been busted. How am I going to wiggle out of this without looking stupid!
5. How could I have produced a better outcome? Changing my internal state to understanding, pushing my ego aside. I could have just said. "Ah really sorry. We probably should have waited to be seated."

Technique for observing yourself: Ego Neutralizer

These are the questions I ask myself, to observe myself when something is at conflict internally.

- Ask yourself how you are feeling (e.g. I am feeling angry)
- Ask yourself why specifically you are feeling the way you do (e.g. I am angry because ...)
- Ask yourself how you are presenting yourself to others when you have this feeling (e.g. Unpleasant, uncaring ...)
- Ask yourself what you said to yourself just before you felt this feeling (e.g. This is not fair ...)
- Ask yourself what you could have said instead (e.g. This is unexpected, but I can make a better choice than feeling angry)

I have used this technique over the past year to evaluate my behaviour in relationships and to evaluate the feelings I project onto others. It is a retrospective technique but can easily be transitioned to the present state by asking yourself the above questions.

Observing yourself is listening to how you feel right now, listening to the thoughts whizzing through your head and listening silently without judgement.

It is in those silences where real self-awareness exists and *You* become separate from your ego. You will begin to realize that *You* are not your emotions. *You* are not your feelings or even your behaviour. Once you accept this, You will see the endless possibilities of *You*.

Do you consider yourself to be self-aware?

Self-awareness is not something that everyone has but I know it can be taught and practised. When you are aware that you are thinking, that awareness is not thinking. It's a silent awareness. Most people will never risk evaluating where they really are. We must know where we are so that we can determine the outcomes that we want.

Self-observation also yields patience. Patience with ourselves. Personal re-invention is centred around patience. We are all preoccupied with instant self-gratification instead of practising being patient. Make time to observe yourself without judgment or self-criticism.

Before we move onto the next chapter, I am going to teach you another simple technique for removing negative emotions from an event that has happened in your life. This technique will fast-track your self-observation skills. Just like that awkward conversation you had when you were out walking the dog, you can remove the feeling from it quickly so there is space to observe your thoughts.

It's called "The Window and Me".

Visualisation Technique for removing negative emotions: The Window and Me

I want you to recall an event which has upset you. What is the level of intensity of this event on a scale of one to ten if you were to know? Maybe your event is a conversation with someone or maybe it was how you responded to someone's behaviour?

I do not want you to be interested in fault, blame or the content of the event. I just want you to feel the feelings that you felt and see yourself inside that situation now.

Are you there? Ok. Good.

Now I want you to see yourself outside a window looking into a room where the event is taking place. You should be able to see yourself in that situation now. If the event took place outside, just put it in a marquee or somewhere inside. Use your imagination.

Now walk backwards one hundred yards from the window. The window is smaller. It is quite a bit harder to see yourself in that room, isn't it?

Do the same again but this time go back five hundred yards. The window itself should be getting more difficult to see.

Now go back nine hundred yards. Can you even see the window?

Keep going back maybe five miles. Nothing should remain of the window.

How do you feel now on a scale of intensity from one to ten?

Repeat this simple process as many times as it takes to get the intensity right down to zero.

This process can be enjoyed more with relaxing music. I would often use *Omvana* for meditation and relaxation. It's an audio app which I use when I want to quieten my mind or have restful sleep. The company behind *Omvana* is MindValley.

Their founder, Vishen Lakhiani, has re-invented himself from being fired at Microsoft to building one of the happiest workplaces in the world with employees in many countries who share his vision. Checkout their YouTube channel.

Use *Omvana* to help you with self-observation and strengthen your *Stop* state.

Observing your thoughts leads to self-control, inner peace and is the foundation for patience, self-love and personal re-invention.

Summary

- Do not limit your life by how *You* see yourself. There is greatness in all of us.
- The purpose of observing yourself is to separate *You* from your ego and gain inner quiet.
- Self-observation is the foundation of personal re-invention and self-acceptance.
- Removing negative emotions surrounding an event will fast-track your self-observation skills.

Techniques

- *Ego Neutralizer* - is a series of questions you can ask yourself to become aware of the feelings which drive your behaviour

- *The Window and Me* - is a visualisation technique for removing negative emotions from an event to enhance your self-observation skills

Useful Resources

- Zig Ziglar is a motivation and personal performance expert. His website is www.ziglar.com. He has a great video on YouTube called <u>Evaluate Where You Are</u>. This video will strengthen your understanding of observing yourself.
- *Eckhart Tolle's* book *A New Earth* provides insight on how to observe our ego. It is available on Amazon.

You can download the resources for this chapter at:

https://go.stopstartreinvent.com/SSR01B1/resources/observe

Patience

Chapter Three

Most people overestimate what they can do in one year and underestimate what they can do in ten years.
- Bill Gates

The Weighing Station

What! I hear you scream. I gotta wait ten years to re-invent my ass? Hell no! I can't possibly wait that long. What'll be the point? Where's the justice in that? I might as well just stay where I am at. It's nice and warm here.

The coffee is good and I don't have to stretch myself. In fact, it's adorably predictable.

I'll still be alive in ten years and won't have had to waste all that energy that all self-developing motivated folk put in. Nah, that's not for me. I could never do that. Besides, I am just big boned. It's not my fault. I have tried to lose weight. I've been to all the meetings. I've tried losing weight with my friend Bernice, running to the weighing station.

Hell, I got so fed up trying to find these different places to go to lose weight, it was adding to my stress. You know, the stress that I have because I am big boned. I realised I had tried my best. My friend told me that some people just can't lose weight. They *are big boned like me. I've been diagnosed as big boned. Those skinny people are so lucky.*

I see them jogging to the park with their sweaty little faces and their energy. I was like that as a kid. It would take me a lifetime to be able to jog to the park. Hell no, that's not for me. I need to stay right where I am.

My doctor says I have high blood pressure because I am big boned. Any exercise could kill me. If I couldn't lose weight the last time I tried, it's sure as hell not gonna happen next time and I am not going to wait ten years to lose it. Oh no. That won't be my game.

That's not for me. Leave that kind of waiting to the skinny folk."

Why do we quit on ourselves?

Change the context but see the form of the above dialogue and you may recognise these kinds of thoughts. These thoughts probably race through your head at break-neck speed. This is an ingrained habit of thinking. It is the thinking that says, "I have something I need to work on" and replies with "I won't be doing that because ..." or says "I would but...."

People often struggle to visualize a version of themselves that is different to their current reality.

First, they don't know how to touch it, feel it or imagine it clearly. They haven't been trained in visualization.

Second, it's an awkward internal conflict. Your ego is concerned with your self-preservation and therefore tries to avoid expending energy or being challenged. So, you are doomed from the outset! Let's all go home and eat chocolate. Right?

Wrong.

Why do so many people quit on themselves?

Why do so many people fail to start, or start and then give up early on?

Why do they fail to maintain consistent effort?

We live in a society which has come to expect everything to appear instantly. We bring our children up to believe in zero work for maximum reward. We don't want them to *suffer* like we did as children. We want them to have everything we didn't and we will go all out to get it.

Generation: Instant

One of my life heroes is Will Smith, not because he is a Hollywood star, but because of his approach to life. One story from an interview of his which has stuck in my head, is from his childhood.

His father knocked down a wall at the shop that they owned. He told Will and his brother to rebuild the wall. They had no idea how to build a wall. How would they do it? It took them a year and a half to rebuild the wall, but they did it. How? They laid a brick at a time perfectly for as long as it took.

Our generation has been lazed through the abundance of technology, sprawling roads and distribution warehouses that can deliver anything next day.

We have come to regard instant as *fitted as standard* in our society. Anything less is not acceptable. We inadvertently apply the same instant gratification to ourselves. We expect instant change to just appear in our life or we give up in frustration and self-defeat.

We don't say "hell yeah, I am going to go all out and have the results I want fitted to me as standard."

No, instead we give up early on with a long list of excuses such as "It will take too long. I won't do it because... I would but..."

Everything will be the same tomorrow, right? Sure, it will, unless you make a conscious effort to change it.

Why is lack of patience detrimental to personal change attempts?

How do you feel if you don't have patience? Think of a time when you felt impatient? If you feel those feelings now and I ask you to recall what it feels like to be frustrated or angry, does it feel similar?

Lack of patience is anger, frustration and resentment in disguise. It's the resentment that the outcome or thing that you do want, has not just landed in your lap. It's the anger that the present situation is not *your* fault. You would get started on your dream, your piano lessons, your weight loss, your business idea, but "I don't live in the right area, I have no time, I have too much to do, I am too tired, my parents didn't help me out."

All these excuses and reasons are your mind's way of deferring responsibility. You are not in charge. You are at the mercy of the reasons behind your present situation.

The internal conflict of believing that you are not the cause of your present circumstances, together with the desire to have a different outcome, leads to impatience.

The Bus and You

I have a question: You are on a bus but where are you sitting? Are you sitting on the front seat, back seat or window seat? Whatever your answer is, the one that gets you the lollipop is, "in the driver's seat". Why? Because subconsciously you want to oversee your own bus, your own direction. So how is this related to patience and personal re-invention?

Personal responsibility is accepting that your present situation is the total sum of the actions you have taken. It's the mindset shift that says "I am not going to be at the effect of life. I am life. I take charge of me. I will battle the storms that come my way, but I will not blame my struggle on the storm, lie down or give up because it has been thrown upon me."

So, the anger, the resentment and frustration that underlies impatience is about personal responsibility.

I want you to really think about this. What is it you've been *trying* to do in your life that you are just getting cross about, frustrated with and therefore have quit more times than you care to mention? Think about it. What are your list of reasons for not doing what you said you would do?

It goes deeper.

I wrote this chapter to share something with you that I learnt about myself at a high price, both personally and financially. Time for you to get to know me a little more. It's not all ice cream and roses in anyone's life!

Too impatient for success

I thought in my early twenties I should be successful and wealthy. Pretty straightforward, right? I reached age twenty-five and realized I was way behind the curve. The years had disappeared. Someone presented a business idea to me. I felt that it would work and I trusted their judgement of the revenue they could attract. I put in about ten thousand pounds of my own money and spent a year building the business.

It failed and the money was irretrievable. The time and the energy spent had not produced any benefit other than teaching me why patience is the foundation of success. In my excitement and impatience at wanting to "make it", I had been listening to my inner voice that was saying jump in, it will be ok. I had not done the due diligence on the venture, the proper market research or accurate costings.

Patience and self-observation of my motivations for engaging in the venture would have changed the outcome dramatically.

Patience is a skill. It must be practised.

Driving at night

This book is my daily practice of patience. It may be a long time before I reach my vision of being able to inspire large groups of people, transform lives and inspire someone at an individual level. I have peace and certainty that if I do something every day towards this outcome, it is worth it.

It will take time, it will be hard, but it will be worth it.

We do not need to know our destination just yet. If you are driving at night your car headlights only shine so far but you trust that the road will keep appearing even though you cannot see all of it. Use this analogy to remind yourself of why we need to learn patience.

You may be wondering, and it's good to wonder, what all this has got to do with your personal re-invention. Is that impatience I hear? Re-read this chapter. I drew your focus to the link between impatience and quitting and then to the link between patience and personal responsibility.

Patience and Motivation

I want to leave you with one last thought. Patience yields motivation. It may sound counter intuitive but patiently taking consistent and regular action, no matter how small, becomes addictive. As humans we are happy when we are progressing.

The small consistent action that you take every day or even every second day, will start to become addictive. These actions become addictive because you start to *like* the feeling of feeling *good*. This feeling of feeling *good* becomes like a drug.

You start to get hooked. You want more. So, you're going to do more to get it. You become motivated and therefore continue taking action so you can enjoy this feeling of *good*.

Patience is a beautiful thing. Master patience and let's move on together.

Summary

- Change the narrative in your head that is keeping you in your same reality by using the same excuses
- Impatience is detrimental to change
- You must be patient in order to build the correct foundations for personal re-invention and ultimately your success
- When you master patience, it will reward you with motivation to go all out and take regular, consistent action

Useful Resources

- Take some time out to listen to Jim Rohn, <u>10 Great Powers</u>
- Will Smith - Watch his interview here about secrets to success. *https://www.youtube.com/watch?v=q5nVqeVhgQE*

You can download the resources for this chapter at:

https://go.stopstartreinvent.com/SSR01B1/resources/patience

Certainty
Chapter Four

Believe in Yourself. Have faith. (Expect to fail).
- John-Paul Byrne, 2015

The quote above is a typical roll off the tongue response you would say to someone who wants to achieve something. The *Expect to Fail* is the unconscious thought we have when we hear these words.

Have faith in yourself?

What? That you will grow an extra arm? Really? C'mon. Faith in yourself has nothing to do with getting what you want, and this chapter is going to kick this destructive thinking from your head.

Self-belief is abstract

Why is it that most people do not achieve the outcomes they want? I am not talking about those people who said, "I am going to be a millionaire and drive a Ferrari." I am talking about you, me or the next-door neighbour. Why do we often not achieve even the smallest of outcomes that we desire?

For instance, "I want to learn Italian", "I want to lose weight", "I want to become a teacher", "I want to ... etc".

Jo: *"I would really like to be able to run a half marathon next year"*.

Liz: *"Really? Wow. Believe in Yourself. Have faith."*

Telling someone to believe in themselves is next to pointless. It means nothing. It's all well intended but it's about as powerful for helping someone succeed as saying nothing at all.

A belief is something that you perceive to be true. So, when we say, "I believe in myself" it's like saying "Yeah, I know I am, I".

Someone can say or even think they believe in themselves but still not achieve the results they want, so what's going on here?

Internally we are relating the words "I believe in myself" to an outcome that we want. There is an expectation that by believing in yourself, the desired outcome will be achieved.

This is a misconception. Self-belief often diverts focus away from the action necessary to achieve the desired outcome.

"I must believe in myself in order to do ...." puts the emphasis on:

- How am I going to believe in myself?
- What is it about me that I don't believe in?
- If I am not able to believe in myself then I cannot achieve the outcome. Oh no. I must believe in myself first, otherwise I cannot even start.

- I must constantly re-evaluate the belief in myself whilst working towards the outcome so I can reassure myself that I can get there.
- Oh no, I feel really crap today. I don't feel good about myself. Do I believe in myself anymore? No. I am going to fail. I am giving up on *that* outcome now because I don't believe in myself anymore.

A sequoia tree, the tallest tree in the world, doesn't go through this chaos. In fact, I am certain of it. It will just be one of the tallest trees. It knows it will be. You are certain about that now aren't you?

We start to see that the "I believe in myself" paradigm is obstructive to getting the outcomes we want. The concept of self-belief always requires an internal evaluation of the concept. An internal determination of what it means to the individual; a determination which is affected by current emotions.

Saying "I believe in myself" is an all-encompassing statement about one's feelings of peace, contentment, pride, joy, love and all those internal representations of self. Mix in a bit of guilt, anger, resentment, hurt and then the likelihood of saying "Yep. I truly believe in myself" seems improbable. It would be lost within the background noise of "I am not perfect. I feel hurt. I feel guilty. They said. I said......"

Self-belief requires plenty of internal clean up that can keep you busy with a therapist. Do you expect to knock all that internal chaos on the head in an instant, so you can lose a few pounds at the gym to feel sexier?

This is going to shock you, but:

There is no need to "believe in yourself" to get the outcomes you want. Instead, just be certain that the outcome is possible for you, provided you input the required action.

<u>Technique for certainty: A Certain Outcome</u>

I want to share a powerful re-frame about "believing in yourself".

How much easier would it be to decide right now that you can be certain of achieving an outcome you desire?

How would you like to put aside the feelings and judgments that you have of yourself?

- Decide to set an outcome for yourself to smile at least once tomorrow
- How certain are you that this outcome is possible?
- How intense is your certainty on a scale of one to ten? If it's not near ten, ramp it up. It's likely isn't it?
- Now that you are feeling certain about smiling tomorrow, ask yourself: "Do you need to believe in yourself to achieve this outcome?"

Now that you have done this activity you have just proved to yourself that you can get an outcome without the need for self-belief.

Certainty got me results

Personal re-invention is not dependent on whether you believe in yourself or not. I am certain of this. You can just let go of the belief that you need to believe in yourself to achieve the results you want.

I can categorically tell you, I do not believe in myself. I am certain of the results I can produce. I have no concept of what believing in myself even means. When I was sleeping rough as a result of being forced to leave my home as a teenager, I was certain I would achieve the highest qualifications in my school.

I did.

When I was going to sell software to a client, I was certain that I would make the sale. I did because it was possible.

When I was a severely depressed and ready to end it all, did I believe in myself? No. Was I certain that it would pass? Yes.

Certainty is free and easy to have. You just decide to be certain of getting the outcome that you want. That's it. There is no need to re-run your internal representation of what self-belief means.

Self-belief is an abstract concept, but certainty is a logical conclusion that something is possible based on the actions you take.

Story: The Red Hammer

Think back to when you were young. The grown-ups would ask "what do you want to be when you are older?" There is one common thread in the answer from every child. The answer is certainty.

Has the child ever heard of "believe in yourself, have faith in yourself"? Probably not. The child is just certain that they can become what they say they will.

Simple really.

Take a moment, close your eyes and take yourself back to the very first ideas you had of what you wanted to do when you were older. See yourself as a child, perhaps in your house or in your school classroom. What was it you wanted to be?

How good did it feel to share your certainty of the future?

When I closed my eyes, I remembered back to when it was Christmas day. No idea what age I was but who cares. Santa had delivered me a wooden toolbox. It was quite large, large enough to sit in. I was very pleased with myself. It had a real hammer inside.

The head of the hammer was painted a glossy red underneath. I was very proud of it. It meant I was free to bang a ridiculous number of nails into just about anything I could find and then hide all the damage in the great big toolbox.

Awesome! Life was good. I proudly announced that I was going to be a carpenter. I loved wood and all I wanted to do was cut, hammer, bang, scrape and do all the fun stuff which boys like to do. I was certain I would be a carpenter.

A compelling reason

What if you are not certain about losing five pounds by going to the gym? What do you do then?

Let's pretend that in thirty days' time, if you have not lost five pounds in weight, you will be given a year's imprisonment.

You are still not certain that you can lose five pounds, are you?

But you now have a "must", a compelling reason to achieve the outcome of weight loss. It's not an option not to lose five pounds in thirty days for you now because the alternative of going to prison is too painful to even consider as an option. It's not even a backup plan.

So, let's recap - why do so many people fail to achieve the outcomes they want? Because they were not *certain* and they didn't have a *must*. That's it. So, what is your *must* going to be if you are not ready to be *certain* right now?

A reason why

My *must* is to complete this book, to talk, to inspire, to guide, to teach, to share.

My *must* is to stay out of depression. The alternative puts me at high risk of spiralling, focusing on the inward.

My *must* is a matter of happiness and peace; the *must* to be in an excellent internal state and to be the best version of me that I can be for my children.

My *must* is to be the best version of me that is possible in order to impact other people's lives in a positive way. It's the *must* to be alive and live a life.

The alternative is too painful. It's not even a backup plan.

You have just moved a mountain. You now have a simple shortcut to getting the results that you want. You are getting stronger, motivated, excited and mentally prepared in exactly the right way so that you are ready to start your personal re-invention.

We have a little more ground to cover in the *Stop* state, but you are here, you are a part of this now. You are addicted to the feelings of good. You may not have expected to feel good until you got started.

I am certain you are going to use this book to get the outcomes you want. You are awesome. You are certain of that now.

Summary

- Self-belief is an abstract concept that must be evaluated internally and is affected by emotions and circumstance.

- Self-belief is a concept that is installed after childhood and is not innate in our thinking. Logical deduction is however.
- Certainty is a logical conclusion that the outcome you want is possible provided you input the necessary action.
- Many people fail to achieve the outcomes they want because they were not *certain* and they didn't have a *must*.

Techniques

- *A Certain Outcome* - this technique installs a new pathway in your brain so you can be certain of achieving an outcome without requiring self-belief.

Useful Resources

- You and Me. We are the only ones who have scrapped ideas about self-belief for certainty!

You can download the resources for this chapter at:

https://go.stopstartreinvent.com/SSR01B1/resources/certainty

Fear
Chapter Five

When you go out and help somebody else, you realize you have no problems.
- Tony Robbins

Do you recognize these self-talks? "I would love to become a singer but I am scared people might laugh at me. I would love to share with others what I know but I am scared people will judge me.

I would love to advise people on my area of expertise but I am scared I don't know enough. What if people think I am no good? What if I fail? What if my friends and family discourage me and tell me I am being stupid?

The fears we have

Fear of pain, fear of negative feelings, fear of rejection, fear of being excluded from a social group, all prevent a person from taking action. If you think of someone successful who you know, ask yourself:

How did they get rid of their fear and take action?

How did they get rid of their fear and step outside their circle of comfort?

The answer is they didn't.

Every person you consider having "made it" has fears. Fear of failure. Fear of making the wrong decision. Fear of losing what they have achieved. Fear of not progressing further. The list goes on.

So, what separates them from the people who haven't got the outcomes they want? They have translated their fears into "musts" by creating a self-talk that begins with "I must do this because..."

The biggest thing holding you back right now is your fears. Freedom is often a word we hear associated with repressed people. It is not something which you might think about on a personal level. Fear of failure is oppressive. Your internal voice that has been saying "I cannot do or be ..." literally chains you and imprisons you. Fear takes away your freedom.

Our internal voice keeps piping up with negativity and pitfalls whenever we try and persuade ourselves that we can achieve the outcomes we want. We discussed this voice, the ego, in the last chapter.

It's the risk manager hell bent on survival with little interest in your stardom. People who get the results they want manage this voice to their advantage.

What do we do when we feel fear?

We think that we have already lost. We relate the feeling of fear to some seemingly inevitable failure. The fear becomes a non-starter.
- John-Paul Byrne 2015

Unlimited Possibility

On the other side of your fear is unlimited possibility. On the other side of your fear is freedom. We need to be able to walk past our fears and focus on what we really want for ourselves.

Without a strategy for dealing with fear, we are going struggle early on in our personal re-invention. We should expect to acquire new fears as we progress, so we need a simple strategy to prevent them from derailing our plans.

I am going to teach you a simple technique to translate every fear you have into a *must*, a driver for personal change that compels you to take action.

This translation will provide the answers to keep your internal voice in check.

Technique for creating "musts": Walk Past Your Fears

Think of something you want to achieve that you are afraid to do. Keep it simple. Take a minute to list some of your fears. Leave a blank line under each one. You will need that space in a moment.

Here are my fears about an online retail business I would like to start:

- It will cost too much money.
- It is going to require time and effort to learn how to do it and I could make mistakes
- I will have less time to spend with my children.

Now write down an alternate fear to the ones you have listed above. An alternate fear is a fear that if you do not do something then you will get an undesired outcome. The undesired outcome should be far *worse* than the original fear.

It's *this* far more painful undesired outcome that is going to compel you to take action and walk past the fears you have listed.

Here are my alternate fears to those that I shared with you above.

- *Fear:* It will cost too much money.

    Alternate: I will be leaving a lot of money on the table by not selling online. This "lost" money will be far greater than my original investment.

- *Fear:* It's going to require time and effort to learn how to do it and I could make mistakes

    Alternate: Not knowing how to do this means I cannot pass on this knowledge to other people and inspire them to have an entrepreneurial spirit.

- *Fear:* I will have less time to spend with my children.

    Alternate: If I do not increase my wealth, I will never be able to spend the time with them I want.

So, what have we done here?

We have completely replaced our fears with motivating *musts*. In fact, the alternative fears are really motivators to work toward what you want and not fears at all.

The alternatives are an answer to the internal negative voice. So, every time you hear your fearful thoughts, consider the alternative and make it a *must*. If you cannot find a *must* then it may not be a strong enough desirable outcome for you.

Story: A Song in My Head

I would like to share a story with you about how I used the *Walk Past Your Fears* technique to make a personal breakthrough.

I found myself alone on Christmas Day 2014.

My relationship had ended with my partner and my children had returned to their Mum's for the rest of the day. There was a thirty minute or so period when I fumbled around the house and felt sorry for myself. I had been invited to a friend's house but for some reason I had decided not to go. Something amazing happened to me.

I asked myself one question.

"What could I do today that could make a difference to at least one person?"

I decided to record a song that I had written a few weeks earlier and put it on YouTube and social media.

Why?

I wanted to raise awareness of homelessness on Christmas Day and draw attention to some of the charities that do excellent work and encourage donations for them. There was one problem. I was scared about anybody listening to my singing. I was even more scared about plastering it all over social media and looking a complete fool.

I translated these fears into alternative compelling *musts*, just like we did earlier. The alternative fear of not making a difference to anyone on Christmas Day was far worse than being an awful singer on social media. I couldn't hand out blankets and food that day so I did what I could with what I had.

I recorded the song in an hour and I edited the video to get my message out. The rest of the evening I promoted it as much as I could on social media. It got two hundred views. Not Adele's standard but two hundred people received my message.

What made it all worthwhile was a man called Kevin who messaged me back and said it had really made him think about how lucky he was. He told me he had donated to one of the charities.

By walking past my fears, I had made a difference.

I later took the opportunity to sing at a band night. This was something I would never have done before. Walking past my fear enabled me to do this and be proud of my music.

Imagine what walking past your fears will enable you to do?

You are a being of unlimited possibility.

The Universal Fear

I want to talk about one fear we all have:

"What will they/he/she/them think of me?"

The fear of being isolated, rejected, ridiculed, unloved or not being accepted is in all of us. But what if you were to allow yourself to accept something?

It's the simplest, logical thing you already know. It will ensure you never have to worry what someone thinks of you again.

Are you ready?

> *You cannot control someone else's thoughts.*
> *- Rob Moore, Progressive Property, Peterborough*

There. That was simple.

Keep moving forward

We are still in our *Stop* state. I hope you are enjoying yourself. I know you will be gaining value from the techniques you are learning. You might wonder why these chapters are titled with just a single word?

These words are what I constantly pull myself back to when I want to achieve anything in my life. I am pulling myself back to them now.

We have discovered how to *observe* ourselves, understand what *patience* is and how it relates to us. We have also learned about *certainty* in getting the outcomes we want and a strategy for dealing with *fear*. These are simple topics relevant to all of us.

You have educated yourself in these areas. You are undertaking valuable self-development. You have empowered yourself by learning simple strategies. You now have a simple strategy to deal with fear. Another mental resource in the arsenal of your amazing mind.

Summary

- People who have achieved the outcomes they wanted translated their fears into compelling "musts".
- Beyond your fears is a version of you with unlimited possibility.
- Walking past your fears is essential to re-inventing yourself.
- We cannot control what other people think of us.

Techniques

- *Walking Past Your Fears* is a technique for creating compelling "musts" enabling you to take action in the direction of your desired outcomes.

Useful Resources

- You can listen to "Song in My Head" at https://www.youtube.com/watch?v=RtGDYFKaQxM
- Tony Robbins - Unleash the Power Within (book)

You can download the resources for this chapter at:

https://go.stopstartreinvent.com/SSR01B1/resources/fear

Love
Chapter Six

A life without love is a life not worth living.
- Keating McFarland.

Most of us believe that we should find someone to love us. We spend our lives looking for it. Some find that person, some never do. For most who have found that other person "who loves" them, they constantly cross reference "Am I being loved. Am I still loved"?

They have a version of what love looks like in their head and cross reference it with what they believe it should feel like, act like, seem like. For others, the proof of love is in the constant testing of the other. The proof of "being loved" becomes a tick sheet where the needs of one is tallied against the giving, the actions of the other "who says they love me".

What is love? Baby don't hurt me.

The only relationships that ever succeed are those in which the participants do not want or need anything of the other. These relationships are built on a shared presence. A shared sense of 'being' when they are together. An unspoken looking outward at the individuality of each other's journey. This is love.

The individuality, non-dependency and wanting of peace, success, fulfilment and happiness for the other; this is love. The acceptance of the struggles of the other and the awareness to empower the other to work through challenges; this is love.

The recognition that being over-protective, suffocating, or dominant is dis-empowering to the other; maintains a strength in love.

The ego's constant search for evidence of "being loved" is the reason for jealousy, resentment and anger. The ego wants to constantly check that it is "being loved" and this can destroy the provider causing the relationship to spiral into negativity. Recognizing this egoistical search maintains self-awareness in love.

The pursuit of happiness

Once I realised that "I am love", I stopped defining myself by a romantic relationship. What we all deeply want is to love somebody else. We do not need someone to love us, instead our true purpose is to give love and be at peace and love oneself as a conscious being. Accepting the fleeting, temporary nature of our time here, has enabled me to recognize that the pursuit of someone "to love me" is futile.

The pursuit of giving my love to someone else is peaceful and brings me happiness.

I have had two serious relationships. Without these relationships, I would of course, not be able to share with you the words above. For me, everything has been learning. Forgiveness of myself for the mistakes I have made has enabled me to move forward. Recognizing the greatness of the others and understanding that we are all doing the best we can with what we have, is part of love.

Forgive Who?

Learning to forgive others is loving yourself.

Forgiveness is giving up the hope that the past could be any different
- Anon

If you are in a place of pain in your life, visit YouTube and watch some of the Oprah Winfrey Life Classes. I found them inspiring and helpful toward understanding myself.

Forgiving others is about forgiving yourself. It's about loving yourself enough to let go of what has gone before and move on.

You do not have to tolerate the wrong doings of others but you can forgive them and yourself. Forgiveness is a gift of freedom for yourself. It's a gift of moving on, not holding someone back, releasing your old thoughts and embracing the present.

It is inevitable that a large part of our personal re-invention is knitted in with our relationships. The relationship we have with ourselves, our partner, husband/wife, friends, family, co-workers. Sometimes we need to take a step outside our closest relationships and ask some tough questions and make some honest observations.

The purpose of doing this is to put your closest relationship into perspective and to evaluate how this impacts you on your road to personal re-invention.

<u>Defining relationships</u>

I realised that I had spent my entire life defining myself by my closest relationship. When I was younger, I lived with my Mum and I defined my self-worth and the internal representations of myself by her feedback. Parents are most likely to do this for you.

As I grew up, every romantic relationship was incredibly intense. I used to think that I could go through my entire life without hurting anyone (this excluded myself). How wrong I was! It seems inevitable that we all hurt someone through our behaviour or words; this is the journey, the experience of life.

It's all temporary so pick up the learning and move on. You went through the good and the bad for learning. It makes you a better you.

You may be reading this book following the breakup of a relationship. The experiences I have had, I hope, will help you gain clarity on your relationship.

<u>Story: Poor Me!</u>

Following my divorce and then the breakup of a three-year-relationship, my world fell apart. I was at the top of the stairs. The house was empty. It was just me. It didn't matter if I screamed, cried or laughed. Nobody was coming. There was no point thinking anymore "whatever happens, she is still here, or I am not alone".

It took some deep thinking to realize that I had not shaped a representation of me that was not my relationship, hence no relationship, no me.

It's that start again moment when I realized "oh shit... so I really am responsible for my life now ... I can fall off the shelf and no one will care, or I can get up and create something from all of this nothingness".

This moment made me realize that first and foremost, to make any relationship work, I had to live for me. I had to love me and this had to be the basis of my future self. It's not about saying "I am not going to change or there is nothing wrong with me ". No ... instead it's saying:

> *If I cannot love myself and live with myself physically and emotionally, then who can I love and who can I live with?*

The answer to that question is nobody. It is in these times that you discover who you are and shape your representation of self. This is why you are reading this book.

Technique for two: Relationship evaluation

If you are in a relationship and it's heading south, you may find these questions useful. They do not have the credit of saving my relationship but they contributed towards a better understanding and allowed an openness that otherwise would not have happened.

Could you and your partner put them to good use to communicate with each other better?

The questions are:

1. What are the things that I love about you?
2. What are the things that I love about me?
3. What are the things that I love about us?
4. What is the shortest list of requirements I have for a relationship?
5. What behaviours can I not accept from my partner?
6. What are the reasons we conflict?
7. What solutions are there to the reasons we conflict?
8. What is my vision as a member of this partnership?
9. What are the things you said that hurt me for which I forgive you?

A shared vision

Les Brown, a motivational speaker with no formal education, re-invented himself and inspired masses of people to get the results they wanted. I often listen to his material online. One point he makes about relationships is that some couples are living together and dying together. One is waiting for the other one to say it's over. Often the relationship is failing because there is no shared vision.

Why did I write this short chapter?

I wanted to share with you what works for me; my reasoning of love and relationships. The reasoning that enables me to live in the now and not be chained to the past.

The past contains the great stuff which happened and the not so great stuff that took place. This reckoning of love is essential to your personal re-invention. What does *love* mean to you? Love ultimately underpins everything in our existence. Keep digging deep enough and it will underpin your personal re-invention.

Summary

- Our true purpose is to give love to our self and to others. It's not to "be loved".

Techniques

- The relationship evaluation questions can be used to structure communication between you and your partner and move forward together

Useful Resources

- Les Brown (www.lesbrown.com) - listen to his speeches on YouTube for inspiration or buy his book "It's Not Over Until I Win"
- Oprah Winfrey Life Class about forgiveness - https://www.youtube.com/watch?v=jbz5IGjKZe8
- You can download the resources for this chapter at: https://go.stopstartreinvent.com/SSR01B1/resources/love

Lows
Chapter Seven

My focus is to forget the pain, mock the pain, reduce it
- Jim Carey

Les Brown says life is cyclic. Paraphrased from his words that inspire me so much, he says:

Sometimes you are up and sometimes you are down. Sometimes you are happy and sometimes you are sad. Anybody can be positive in the up's when their bills are paid, their relationships are good, the kids are behaving. Anybody can be positive then. You are never just going to have things on an even keel. You are either dealing with a problem, just finished working on one, or you have your next one on order. Problems are life. It is from problems and challenges that we grow.

In writing in this book, I want to share with you this certainty:

There will never be a time in your life when you will reach a consistent, sustainable and unchanging level of happiness. I know you can find happiness in this truth. It is in the darkest hours that the strongest light is forged. In the lowest of times that the real work on yourself is done.
- John-Paul Byrne 2015

Rocky Balboa inspired me with these words.

> *The world ain't all sunshine and rainbows. It is a very mean and nasty place. It will beat you to your knees and keep you there permanently if you let it. You, me or nobody is going to hit as hard as life. But it ain't about how hard you're hit, it is about how hard you can get hit and keep moving forward, how much can you take and keep moving forward. That's how winning is done!*

What's the point?

We all want to be happy. We all want to appear strong around our friends and family. We all want to look like we have it *all going on, all the time.* So, we absolutely must talk about what most people feel embarrassed about, even ashamed of.

I am talking about the lows, the sadness, the depressions, the rough times, those zero energy times.

The "I got no motivation" times.

The quitting times.

The give up times.

The "what's the point times?"

I don't care who you are, what you've learned or where you've come from, you are going to have lows in your life.

Low Labels

Lows will vary in intensity according to the problem. They will vary in intensity according to the beholder. They will vary in intensity according to the resilience, the emotional intelligence and self-awareness of the individual. They will vary in intensity according to the mental health of the person.

For some, depression or lows are a condition just as one might have asthma.

You cannot say to someone "don't have asthma". You cannot say to someone "don't be depressed". You cannot say to somebody, "could you just make your brain make more serotonin right now".

In today's society there are labels for those of us for whom the intensity of the highs and the lows are outside the boundaries of what we expect to be normal. Yet one in four of us will be outside the boundaries of what is expected to be normal at some point in our lives.

One in four of us will suffer with mental health issues. One in four of us will need the mental resources and the self-awareness to know that this depression, this low, has not come to stay, it has come to pass.

Fighting Depression?

If we must use labels, I am Bipolar Type II. I have spent large portions of my life in depression. I have spent a large percentage of my life being awake for twenty-four hours or more, working with seemingly unbounded mental energy yet knowing that in the distance will come the crash, the low.

The low that when you open your eyes in the morning you say to yourself "oh God, am I still alive. I don't want to be alive anymore. I will have to do just one more day." This is the same low that wakes you up in the middle of the night in sheer panic and with an overwhelming sense of isolation. It's those times when you feel there is nothing or no-one right there and then who can help you.

I dislike labels. I dislike the acceptance that poor health is permanent. I dislike giving up on myself when everyone around me has not. I dislike depression.

Do I think depression is survivable?

Yes.

Do I think I can live to my fullest potential?

Yes.

Do I think I could have depression again?

Yes.

Do I resent taking medication because it helps my brain balance its levels of serotonin?

No.

I want to grow from it and capitalize on it; see it as an opportunity and a gift of understanding. It is an opportunity to help others move through it and still achieve the outcomes they want for themselves.

This chapter is for everyone because everyone has lows. Do not fight depression; look for happiness and purpose instead.

There are plenty of far more qualified people than me who can educate you on managing depression or lows.

I want to inspire you to unlock the power you have inside yourself to re-invent your life whether you are at the height of happiness or in the depths of despair. I want to inspire you to live your best *You*.

I want this book on personal re-invention to equip you with the mental resources and the techniques that will see you through those "give up" moments.

> *Whether you have been officially diagnosed as depressed, have the baby blues or just feel sad every third day and have no idea why; You are not your feelings. You are not your depression. You are far more than this. Accepting this is courage.*
> *- John-Paul Byrne*

The Depressed Mind

In my experience, the two commonalities in depression are lack of hope and the abdication of rescuing self. When the human mind has no hope, it does not want to carry on and has no vision of a future that is beyond the current experience of pain.

The depressed mind judges the present situation as that which is here to stay. The depressed mind is resigned to the depression and finds it easy to fall further and further downwards. The depressed mind will not accept that it has been here before and that the depression has ended before.

One of the turning points for me was the realization that nobody else can fix it or ease it but me. During depression there is often confusion because there is a hope that someone will be able to rescue us and ease the pain. This hope is conflicting because of the feelings of wanting to "give up".

There are amazing people out there who stick by those in their darkest times. Their journey, their watching and their patience is something that takes great strength of character and love.

Watching, waiting, understanding while someone you love is depressed is a very difficult role to play.

Roses and Lollipops

So why are we talking about depression and lows? The last part of our *Stop* state is to be certain that life is not going to be consistently happy. Your driving force for wanting to re-invent your life should not be the attainment of *consistent* happiness.

Expect tough times.

If you are prone to depression or lows, expect that they may re-occur. That's ok. Be upfront and honest with what you have that might try to knock you off your path. This is not some bullshit read by someone who is telling you it's going to be all roses and lollipops. This is you accepting that today you might be firing on all cylinders, feeling motivated, strong, clear minded and focused but tomorrow you might want to quit, give up, end it or cry.

You might want to beat yourself up when you miss three days of training because you are really depressed and couldn't get out of bed. That's ok. It's what you are working with.

What's not ok is to be under-prepared for the tough times. You need to have resources in your physical world around you that are going to remind you that this depression will not last. So how are you going to do that?

Technique for dealing with depression or sadness: Send Yourself a Message

This technique is to help you remind yourself that the next time you are feeling low, it will not last forever.

If there is one message you could send your tomorrow self, what would it be?

When I feel strong, motivated and I am taking the consistent action towards the outcomes that I want, I leave myself notes. I used to leave post-it notes around the house. I would stick phrases and thoughts on the walls.

When the low starts to kick in, I accept it. I take some time out. I recognize that a break is needed. The machine, the body, the mind is saying: "I can't deal with anymore right now. I am all maxed out to capacity."

I stop.

You can do this too.

In that state of stillness I rest and wait, knowing that what I feel today is not what has come to stay.

Looking Low

It would be great if we could see depression. It would be great if it was so widely understood and accepted that you could say to someone "I am feeling really low and I have no idea why" just the same way you might say "I have a headache". We may perceive feeling depressed or low as weakness, which is ironic considering we are spiritual and emotional beings.

All that aside, it doesn't really matter what the outside world perceives as your state of happiness internally. What matters is that you are honest with yourself and taking the necessary steps to cope in the hard times, building your resilience and preparing yourself with messages, tools and support. This is going to remind you that any depression or low will end and that you will come out the other side ready to continue.

Moving forward, looking back

How far have we come?

This is the last chapter in our *Stop* state. Could you tell someone the important messages that you gained from the previous chapters?

What is it about this learning that has changed you?

Where are you now that you were not when you opened this book?

Do you know your *Stop* state or are you just speed reading so you say you have read this book?

We have talked about how to enter the *Stop* state, how to observe yourself, turn patience into motivation, belief into certainty, fear into "musts", love into happiness and lows into progress.

Why?

Because these are all the aspects I have been through to re-invent myself. These are all the concepts that I have embraced which allow me to move forward.

In the next book in this series, **Start: Begin Your Personal Re-Invention Today**, you will be defining your purpose and taking action.

I don't care what you want to change, anything is possible.

It is necessary that you have a dream.
It is necessary that you have purpose.

> *I have not come this far to quit. This is my dream,*
> *my mission and I am going all out to have it.*
> *- John-Paul Byrne*

Summary

- Life is cyclic so you will never be consistently happy or consistently sad.
- One in four of us will suffer with depression or lows. The labels do not matter because it's the resources you give yourself to manage it that count.
- You are not your feelings. You are not your depression. You are far more than this.

Techniques

- *Send Yourself a Message* is a technique for dealing with depression or sadness. You send yourself a message that you can refer to when you are feeling low and remind yourself that your present state of mind is not here to stay.

Useful Resources

- A pen and post-it notes. Write down what was good about today. Keep it safe.

You can download the resources for this chapter at:

https://go.stopstartreinvent.com/SSR01B1/resources/lows

Get Ready To START
Chapter Eight

I am so happy that you are on this journey with me. I would love for you to continue it right through to the end. Please make a commitment to yourself as I have committed to *You* by authoring this three-part series. I made this commitment to myself so *You* and others, could embark on a journey of lasting life change.

You might just be the person reading or listening to this book, who is that one special person who finds happiness, relief and success through these words.

I wrote **STOP. START. RE-INVENT** back in 2015 and yet I write this final chapter in part-one of this series, here in 2020.

Why?

As you can see, the book was not published in 2015. It's taken five years to bring it to publication. I wanted to leave all chapters unchanged, as I wrote them in 2015.

My wish for you is to see my journey right to the end of the last and third book in this series. Within that last book you will see the completion of my own personal re-invention and the lessons contained within.

Ensure you read all the books in order. Don't be tempted to skip to end. One thing you can be sure of though is that I am a published author of multiple books. That is a sneak peek at some of my personal re-invention. There is so much more that has happened to me since, both consciously and unconsciously.

I can't wait to reveal all the pain, challenges, success and realisations that have brought me to this point as I sit in my chair, on a Saturday morning in my dressing gown, writing this chapter to you.

Stick with me. This will be beautiful.

Author Summary

Creating the change you want to see in your life is not always easy. We are programmed to run to shiny objects hoping they will be the solution we have needed all along.

Yet we so often find ourselves right back where we started, wondering where it all went wrong. The more this cycle repeats for people, the more disheartened they become and the more they condition themselves to accepting their life as it is. Eventually they become stuck in negative thoughts, chronic dissatisfaction and living half a life while feeling a victim of it.

There is so much potential in people to be happier and have their life the way they want it, yet it is often never achieved. When people are in despair, unhappy with their life or looking to create change, they often go searching for books or programs that teach how to become successful, wealthy or start a business.

Typically, the world conditions those who want change, to believe that the change they need is huge success, money and recognition beyond the ordinary everyday life.

I think this is a real failing of our self-help world because many people feel that they need to make massive life changes in order to simply change and enjoy this human experience to its fullest.

So, my message to you is this:
Improve Your Life. Live Your Best You.

Remember that your personal re-invention is always personal to you. Don't try and write a conventional story of success. Write your own story that is a commitment to the lasting change that you want for *your* life.

One of my big life lessons was learning to stop and reflect on my thoughts, beliefs and values. All too often, I found myself jumping from one thing to the next, never actually stopping to re-evaluate.

Weirdly, as I write this author summary now in 2020, I am in a STOP state.

Why?

Because I have begun another journey of personal re-invention having completed the personal re-invention that I started in 2015.

I wrote this book and the other two books in the series, to inspire you to re-invent your life.

Acknowledgements

Thank you to everyone in my life who has treated me with kindness and compassion. There are many people I would like to thank who have supported me.

They have given me constant love and kindness and I am truly grateful to them as I doubt I would have made it through at times.

Thank you to Flavia for your love, kindness and encouragement to discover myself and never give up. Your belief in me and constant reminder of my core being has enabled me to begin to fly and love myself. Thank you for the endless hours of listening, patience and guidance and for never judging my anger and confusion and instead helping me towards inner peace. You are a beautiful soul and I have beautiful memories with you that I will always treasure.

Thank you to my wonderful friends, Chris, Mel, Nick and Isy who have always been there to pick me up everytime I fell into a dark place. Your love, guidance, non-judgemental and balanced attitude has enabled me to feel safe and reminded me that whatever I go through, it's going to be OK and I will prevail.

To my beautiful children Bobby and Bethany, you are both a gift from the universe. You have come through your Mum and I and bring us joy and laughter everyday. I can see in you both, kindness, love and compassion. I am so proud of you, not because of your achievements, but because of who you truly are. I will always be here to guide you, love you and help you on your soul journey. Nothing you do is ever wrong, it's all learning and growth.

To my ex-wife Kay for your constant love even when I treated you terribly. You never ever returned anger or hate and always looked upon me with kindness and compassion, even when I lost the plot. You are the most forgiving and understanding soul I have ever met and I am truly grateful for you being in my life. You never judged me and have provided endless guidance every time I mess up. You protected me from others judgment and understood my mental health challenges with love and compassion. Thank you for our beautiful children and being a wonderful Mum.

To my Dad and Marianne for your love, guidance, acceptance and understanding. You are my parents and I love you dearly. You always say the right thing and encourage me to grow. Thank you for being so wonderful.

Thank you to my mental health professionals and therapists. To Tamsin, Graham and Eleanor for your therapy, skill and knowledge that helped me understand my ADHD, Bipolar Disorder, RSD and everything in between. Without you I would still be a victim of my childhood trauma. You made me feel safe and gave me the pathway to recovery and growth.

To the people who have been in my life; my clients, partners, friends and business associates who have treated me with understanding and faith. I have learned much from you all.

Thank you to You, the reader, for trusting me with my experience and knowledge and taking the time to listen or read my words. You give me a real sense of purpose and value by purchasing my books. I hope they help you immensely.

Thank you to myself, John-Paul, my higher being for guiding me on this sometimes harrowing, often beautiful, soul journey and physical experience.

Thank you.

About the Author

John-Paul Byrne is an author, international speaker, coach, CEO of Communicator Dynamics© and creator of Man of Emotion©.

He writes books on mental health, self-development, business & entrepreneurship, linguistics & communication, science fiction and spirituality.

His core message across all his work is:

"Improve Your Life. Live Your Best You".

You can discover more about him at

www.JohnPaulByrne.com

Originally from the Republic of Ireland, he now lives in the UK with his two young children. Despite a long career in software development, he has turned to writing as a passion project.

Within his words, he talks to You, the reader, as he would a friend enjoying a conversation.

In this book he shares his own personal experiences, thoughts, strategies and ideas for creating lasting change in your life, mental health and personal growth.

He has *Bipolar Disorder (BP)* and *Attention Deficit Hyperactivity Disorder (ADHD)* but refuses to limit his life or submit to these labels as permanent, incurable or unchangeable. He embraces the gifts that come with these conditions, one of which is creativity.

   He has a keen interest in personal development, mindset and the effects of brain dysfunction.

Life doesn't need to be perfect. It just needs to be true.
- John-Paul Byrne 2020

Get Book #2

in the
STOP. START. RE-INVENT series

Thank you for putting your faith in me and purchasing this book.

STOP: Get Ready To Re-Invent Yourself is the first book in the series **STOP. START. RE-INVENT: How To Re-Invent Yourself & Create Lasting Change In Your Life**

The next book in this series is called:

START: Begin Your Personal Re-Invention Today

Please visit the link below to get your copy of the second book in this series in either paperback, kindle or audible formats

https://go.stopstartreinvent.com/SSR01B2/buy

I would be most grateful if you could leave a review on Amazon so that others looking to make lasting change in their life can benefit from this series.

I wish you inner peace, joy and enthusiasm
as you embark on your personal re-invention

- John-Paul Byrne, Peterborough, UK

Leave a Review

I would be so grateful if you could help others looking to make lasting change in their life by writing a review for this book on Amazon.

Other Books In This Series

Book #2

Book #2: START: Begin Your Personal Re-Invention Today
https://go.stopstartreinvent.com/SSR01B2/buy

Book #3

Book #3: RE-INVENT: Strategies For Lasting Change And Personal Growth

https://go.stopstartreinvent.com/SSR01B3/buy

Appendix

Other books available in the series ***STOP. START. RE-INVENT: How To Re-Invent Yourself & Create Lasting Change In Your Life*** are available at

www.StopStartReInvent.com

or on Amazon from my author page

https://go.johnpaulbyrne.com/amazon

Printed in Great Britain
by Amazon